# What Do You Know About Bugs?

## Understand Place Value

Alana Olsen

**PowerKiDS** press™

NEW YORK

Published in 2015 by The Rosen Publishing Group, Inc.
29 East 21st Street, New York, NY 10010

Book Design: Mickey Harmon

Photo Credits: Cover Brian Chase/Shutterstock.com; p. 5 (ladybug) PHOTO FUN/Shutterstock.com; p. 5 (cicada) Smit/
Shutterstock.com; p. 5 (cricket) Mark Bridger/Shutterstock.com; p. 5 (mosquitoes) Dieter H/Shutterstock.com;
p. 7 Natursports/Shutterstock.com; p. 9 smuay/Shutterstock.com; p. 11 Dmitrijs Bindemanis/Shutterstock.com;
p. 13 alexsvirid/Shutterstock.com; p. 15 Yuriy Kulik/Shutterstock.com; p. 17 (dog-day cicada) Julie C. Wagner/
Shutterstock.com; p. 17 (17-year cicada) Jason Patrick Ross/Shutterstock.com; p. 19 Denis Tabler/Shutterstock.com;
p. 21 inxti/Shutterstock.com; p. 22 StudioSmart/Shutterstock.com.

Library of Congress Cataloging-in-Publication Data

Olsen, Alana, author.
 What do you know about bugs? : understand place value / Alana Olsen.
     pages cm. — (Math masters. Number and operations in base ten)
 Includes index.
 ISBN 978-1-4777-4663-9 (pbk.)
 ISBN 978-1-4777-4664-6 (6-pack)
 ISBN 978-1-4777-6431-2 (library binding)
 1. Place value (Mathematics)—Juvenile literature. 2. Mathematics—Juvenile literature. 3. Insects—Juvenile literature. I.
Title.
 QA141.3.O47 2015
 513.2′1—dc23
                                        2013042846

Manufactured in the United States of America

CPSIA Compliance Information: Batch #WS15RC: For further information contact Rosen Publishing, New York, New York at 1-800-237-9932.

# Contents

So Many Bugs!                            4

Mosquito Facts                           6

Noisy Bugs                              12

Learning About Ladybugs                 18

Helpful Bugs                            22

Glossary                                23

Index                                   24

# So Many Bugs!

Did you know that there are more bugs on Earth than people? There are millions of species, or kinds, of bugs that live all over the world. Some bugs are helpful. They eat pests that can destroy crops. Other bugs carry illnesses that can be **harmful** to people and other animals. Can you name any helpful or harmful bugs?

One million (1,000,000) is the same as 1,000 thousands. **Scientists** believe there are still millions of bug species waiting to be discovered and studied!

# Mosquito Facts

One kind of bug with many species living in North America is the **mosquito**. There are at least 170 mosquito species in North America. How many ways can you write the number 170? You can use its number name to show that the number is "one hundred seventy." You can also add the number of hundreds, tens, and ones.

170 = one hundred seventy
170 = 1 hundred + 7 tens + 0 ones
170 = 100 + 70 + 0

When you show a number as ones, tens, and hundreds added together, you're showing the number's expanded form.

Most bugs come from eggs. Girl mosquitoes lay their eggs on water. The eggs float on the water and stick together in groups of 100 or more. If there was a group made up of 115 mosquito eggs, you could use expanded form to show how big that number is. The number is made of 1 hundred, 1 ten, and 5 ones.

115 = one hundred fifteen
115 = 1 hundred + 1 ten + 5 ones
115 = 100 + 10 + 5

After mosquitoes hatch, or break out of their eggs, they live
in the water until they grow their wings.

Mosquitoes have wings that beat very quickly. Some girl mosquitoes can beat their wings 250 to 500 times per second! If 1 mosquito beats its wings 342 times per second, that number can be broken down using expanded form. It would be written as 300 + 40 + 2 because it's made up of 3 hundreds, 4 tens, and 2 ones.

342 = 3 hundreds + 4 tens + 2 ones
342 = 300 + 40 + 2

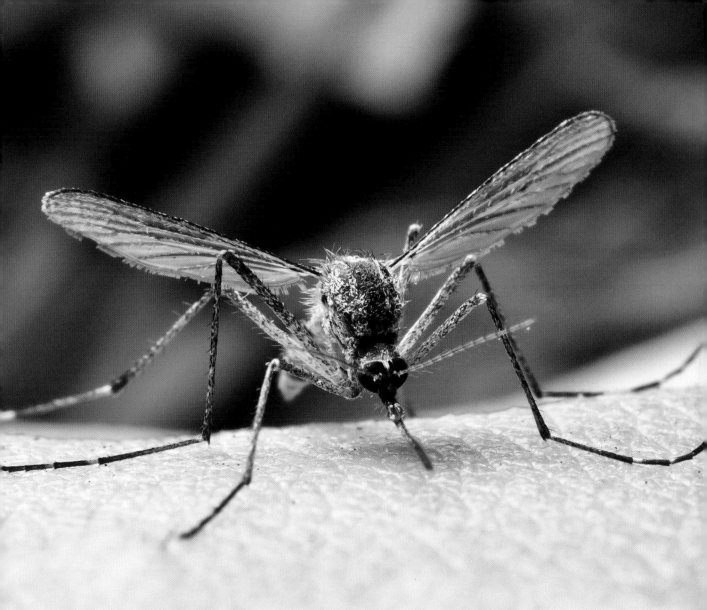

Girl mosquitoes beat their wings so quickly because boy mosquitoes are **attracted** to the buzzing sound it makes.

# Noisy Bugs

Many other bugs use their wings to make noise, too. A cricket makes a chirping sound by rubbing one wing against a row of teeth on the other wing. There can be as many as 250 teeth on a cricket's wing. If a cricket has 212 teeth on its wing, how would you write that number using words?

$$212 = 200 + 10 + 2$$

Using its number name, 212 is written
as "two hundred twelve."

Cicadas (suh-KAY-duhz) are bugs that are known for making loud buzzing noises. The noises come from their abdomen (AB-duh-muhn), or the middle part of their body. Boy cicadas make noises that can be as loud as 120 decibels. A decibel is a **unit** used to measure how loud a sound is, and 120 decibels is as loud as a rock concert!

120 = one hundred twenty

The number 120 can be shown in expanded form
as 100 + 20 + 0.

Cicadas are also known for disappearing for long periods of time. The dog-day cicada is only seen in the "dog days" of summer, which is a name sometimes used for the middle of summer. The 17-year cicada got its name from the fact that it only appears every 17 years after spending most of its life underground. How can you show the number 17 using expanded form?

17 = 1 ten + 7 ones
17 = 10 + 7

dog-day
cicada

17-year
cicada

A 17-year cicada is also called a periodical cicada because it's only seen after long periods of time. A dog-day cicada is also called an annual cicada because it's seen annually, or every year.

# Learning About Ladybugs

Most bugs don't live as long as the 17-year cicada. The ladybug is a very common bug in the United States. It's known for its red coloring and black spots. Ladybugs can live for over 2 years in the wild, which is the same as 730 days. What are all the ways you can write the number 730?

730 = seven hundred thirty
730 = 7 hundreds + 3 tens + 0 ones
730 = 700 + 30 + 0

Ladybugs are very helpful bugs. They help control the number of pests on farms, and this keeps crops safe.

Ladybugs are sometimes seen as signs of good luck. They can be found all over the world, and there are over 5,000 species of ladybugs. In California alone, there are at least 175 species of ladybugs. Can you use a number name and expanded form to show the number 175?

175 = ?

There are thousands of species of ladybugs. Using expanded form, 1,000 is shown as 1,000 + 0 + 0 + 0. Using its number name, it's written as "one thousand."

# Helpful Bugs

Bugs are important parts of the natural world. They produce things that people have used throughout history, such as honey (from bees) and silk (from silkworms). There are many different species of bugs in the world. Take a look and listen the next time you're outside, and see if you can guess what bugs are around you!

Bugs help people in many ways, including giving us food to eat and **material** to make clothing.

# Glossary

**attract** (uh-TRAKT)  To cause to come close.

**harmful** (HAARM-fuhl)  Causing hurt or loss.

**material** (muh-TIHR-ee-uhl)  Something from which something else can be made.

**mosquito** (muh-SKEE-toh)  A small, flying bug. Girl mosquitoes have a pointed body part used for sucking the blood of people and other animals.

**scientist** (SY-uhn-tihst)  Someone who studies the way things work and the way things are.

**unit** (YOO-nuht)  A standard amount by which things are measured.

# Index

bees, 22

cicadas, 14, 16, 17, 18

cricket, 12

expanded form, 7, 8, 10, 15, 16, 20, 21

hundreds, 6, 7, 8, 10, 18

ladybugs, 18, 19, 20, 21

millions, 4

mosquitoes, 6, 8, 9, 10, 11

number names, 6, 13, 20, 21

ones, 6, 7, 8, 10, 16, 18

silkworms, 22

species, 4, 6, 20, 21, 22

tens, 6, 7, 8, 10, 16, 18

thousands, 4, 21

Due to the changing nature of Internet links, The Rosen Publishing Group, Inc., has developed an online list of websites related to the subject of this book. This site is updated regularly. Please use this link to access the list: www.powerkidslinks.com/mm/nobt/wabug